To *

From Aunt

Christmas 1995
spent in Washington
with wonderful
family

MW00416961

⅋Christmas Carol

Cookbook

Sarah Key

Jennifer Newman Brazil

Vicki Wells

Abbeville Press Publishers

New York · London · Paris

Designer: Celia Fuller
Production Manager: Matthew Pimm
Copyeditor: Virginia Croft

Special thanks to Kermit Sullivan, Ellen Gray Kennedy, and
Eric and Bruce Bromberg of Blue Ribbon Restaurant.

All photographs courtesy of Turner Entertainment Co. except as follows:
page 2, courtesy Everett Collection; page 24, courtesy The Kobal Collection.

Also available in the Hollywood Hotplates series:

Gone With The Wind Cookbook ™
The Casablanca Cookbook
The Wizard of Oz Cookbook

Cataloging-in-Publication Data
Key, Sarah
     A Christmas Carol Cookbook / Sarah Key, Jennifer Newman Brazil, Vicki Wells.
        p.   cm.
     ISBN 1-55859-584-8
     1. Christmas cookery.   I. Brazil, Jennifer Newman.   II. Wells, Vicki.   III. Title
TX739.2.C45K49 1993
641.5'68—dc20
                                                        93-6090

Metric conversions: 1 teaspoon = 5 ml; 1 tablespoon = 14.8 ml.

Contents

Tea with Marley's Ghost

Traditional English Tea with Tarts, Trifles, and Sundry Sweets

Darkness is cheap, and Scrooge liked it. . . . Quite satisfied, he closed his door, and locked himself in; double-locked himself in, which was not his custom. Thus secured against surprise, he took off his cravat; put on his dressing-gown and slippers, and his nightcap; and sat down before the fire to take his gruel. . . . Upon its coming in, the dying flame leaped up, as though it cried, "I know him; Marley's Ghost!" and fell again.

Scrooge & Marley's Hot Tea

By the Victorian era, tea was no longer just for the aristocracy. Everyone drank tea, and it had become an afternoon ritual. To brew the perfect cup of tea:

1. *Use tea leaves. They are much superior to tea bags.*

2. *Fill a tea kettle with cold water. Bring water to a boil. As soon as water reaches a rolling boil, turn heat off immediately and brew the tea. If water boils too long, it loses oxygen and the tea tastes murky.*

3. *In a teapot, place 1 heaping teaspoon of leaves per cup. Place leaves directly into pot if you have a strainer. Otherwise use a wire or metal tea infuser.*

4. *Pour boiling water directly on leaves. Cover teapot and let steep for 3 to 6 minutes, depending on size of the tea leaves. Small leaves steep the shortest, and large ones the longest.*

5. *Strain tea into cups and serve with lemon or milk and sugar if desired.*

Tea begins with an assortment of tea sandwiches, followed by scones and then pastry. Traditional fillings include cucumber, egg, smoked salmon, chicken, and watercress. Aside from the two recipes here, the potted shrimp (p. 31) and the gravalax (p. 35) also make wonderful fillings for sandwiches that can be served at tea or with cocktails. For any filling, always use very fresh bread. Be careful not to stack the filling too high because, once sliced into fingers, the sandwiches will be difficult to eat. Sandwiches can be sliced into fingers, quarters, or triangles. Fancy tea sandwiches are sometimes made bite size with canapé cutters.

If sandwiches are made ahead, remember that they dry out quickly. To prevent such drying, place prepared sandwiches on a plate, cover with a damp towel, and refrigerate until ready to serve. Also, do not toast bread unless sandwiches are to be served immediately.

Chicken Tarragon Tea Sandwiches

1 ½ boneless skinless chicken breasts (3 chicken breast halves)
salt and freshly ground black pepper
3 tablespoons (42 g) unsalted butter
¾ cup (165 g) prepared mayonnaise
¼ cup (10 g) minced fresh tarragon
18 slices pumpernickel bread
½ bunch watercress, washed and stems removed
3 cucumbers, peeled and thinly sliced

Sprinkle chicken breasts lightly on both sides with salt and pepper. In a large skillet, melt butter over medium-low heat. Add ½ cup (120 ml) cold water and chicken breasts and simmer 7 to 8 minutes on each side or until cooked through. Cooking time will vary according to thickness of chicken breast. Remove chicken from pan and let cool. Combine mayonnaise and tarragon in a small bowl and set aside. Slice each breast into thirds horizontally, producing 9 thin slices each the size of the chicken breast.

Lightly toast bread. Spread 9 slices of toast with 1 tablespoon of tarragon mayonnaise. Top each with a slice of chicken, then cover with watercress leaves and a few slices of cucumber. Top each sandwich with another slice of toast. With a sharp serrated knife, remove crusts. Cut each sandwich into quarters.

Sandwiches must be served the same day they are prepared.

MAKES 36 TEA SANDWICHES.

Egg and Chutney Tea Sandwiches

14 slices white sandwich bread
5 tablespoons (70 g) unsalted butter, at room temperature
¾ cup (225 g) chutney (use prepared chutney or recipe on p. 47)
7 hard-cooked large eggs, thinly sliced

Lightly toast bread. Spread 7 slices of toast with butter. Spread chutney on top of butter, then cover chutney with slices of egg. Top each sandwich with another slice of toast. With a sharp serrated knife, remove crusts and slice each sandwich into thirds.

Sandwiches must be served the same day they are prepared.

MAKES 21 FINGER SANDWICHES.

Orange Scones

2 cups (280 g) all-purpose flour
¼ cup (50 g) sugar
1 tablespoon baking powder
½ teaspoon salt
1 large egg
grated zest of 1 orange (about 2 teaspoons)
¼ cup (60 ml) orange juice
½ cup (120 ml) heavy cream
2 tablespoons orange-flavored brandy
¼ cup (56 g) unsalted butter, melted

Preheat oven to 350°F (180°C). Line a baking sheet with parchment or waxed paper. Sift flour, sugar, baking powder, and salt into a large bowl. In another bowl, whisk together egg, orange zest, orange juice, cream, brandy, and butter. Make a well in dry ingredients and pour egg mixture into well. Slowly stir egg mixture into flour mixture with a wooden spoon or spatula until a dough is formed. Roll or pat dough out on a floured surface to ½ inch (13 mm) thick. Cut out 2-inch (5-cm) rounds with a cookie cutter or glass. Reroll any dough scraps and cut into rounds. Place rounds on lined baking sheet. Brush with a little heavy cream and sprinkle with sugar. Bake on top rack of oven for about 12 minutes. Bottoms will brown lightly but the tops will remain uncolored. Serve warm.

MAKES ABOUT 1½ DOZEN.

Camden Town Bacon and Sage Scones

2 cups (280 g) all-purpose flour
1 tablespoon baking powder
¼ teaspoon salt
¼ teaspoon freshly ground black pepper
1 teaspoon dried sage
⅓ cup (30 g) cooked crumbled bacon
1 large egg
¼ cup (60 ml) bacon drippings
½ cup (120 ml) heavy cream
⅓ cup (80 ml) milk

Preheat oven to 350°F (180°C). Line a baking sheet with parchment or waxed paper. In a large bowl, sift flour, baking powder, salt, and pepper. Rub sage between fingers into flour. Add crumbled bacon and mix well. In another bowl, whisk together egg, bacon drippings, heavy cream, and milk. Make a well in dry ingredients and pour egg mixture into well. Slowly stir egg mixture into flour mixture with a wooden spoon or spatula until a dough is formed.

Roll or pat dough out on a floured surface to ½ inch (13 mm) thick. Cut out 2-inch (5-cm) rounds with a cookie cutter or glass. Reroll dough scraps and cut into rounds. Place rounds on lined baking sheet. Brush with a little bacon drippings or heavy cream. Bake on top rack of oven for about 12 minutes or until very lightly browned. Serve warm.

MAKES ABOUT 1½ DOZEN.

Jacob Marley's Sugar Dough

And then let any man explain to me, if he can, how it happened that Scrooge, having his key in the lock of the door, saw in the knocker, without its undergoing any intermediate process of change—not a knocker, but Marley's face.

1 cup (227 g) unsalted butter, at room temperature
¾ cup (150 g) sugar
¼ teaspoon salt
2 large egg yolks
2 teaspoons vanilla extract
2 ⅓ cups (325 g) all-purpose flour

In an electric mixer or food processor, cream butter, sugar, and salt until light and fluffy. Add yolks and vanilla. Continue to blend until incorporated. Stir in flour by hand with a spatula or wooden spoon. Wrap dough in plastic wrap or aluminum foil. Chill for at least 1 hour. Dough can be stored several days in refrigerator or several months in freezer. Use this recipe to make Scrooge's Lemon Tartlets, Mincemeat Tartlets, and Nectarine Tarts (recipes follow).

Scrooge's Lemon Tartlets

½ recipe sugar dough (preceding recipe)
2 cups (600 g) lemon curd (p. 49)

Roll out dough on a lightly floured surface to ⅛ inch (3 mm) thick. Cut out rounds with a 2-inch (5-cm) cookie cutter. Press dough into 2-inch (5-cm) miniature tart molds. Place on a baking sheet and chill in freezer for 15 minutes or longer. When ready to bake, preheat oven to 350°F (180°C). Place baking sheet with tartlet shells in oven. Bake for 10 to 12 minutes or until dough is golden brown. Let tartlet shells cool. Fill each one with 1 teaspoon lemon curd. Cover until ready to serve.

MAKES 40 2-INCH (5-CM) TARTLETS.

Mincemeat Tartlets

There were more dances, and there were forfeits, and more dances, and there was cake, and there was negus, and there was a great piece of Cold Roast, and there was a great piece of Cold Boiled, and there were mince-pies, and plenty of beer.

2 cups (500 g) mincemeat (p. 52)
½ recipe sugar dough (preceding page)

Follow instructions in preceding recipe for tartlet shells, then fill each with 1 teaspoon mincemeat.

MAKES 40 2-INCH (5-CM) TARTLETS.

Nectarine Tarts

1 recipe sugar dough (preceding page)

Filling
4 large ripe nectarines, halved, pitted, and thinly sliced
1 cup (227 g) sour cream
¼ cup (50 g) sugar
2 tablespoons flour
¼ teaspoon salt
1 teaspoon vanilla extract
1 large egg

Topping
½ cup (120 g) firmly packed brown sugar
¼ cup (56 g) unsalted butter
⅓ cup (45 g) all-purpose flour

Preheat oven to 400°F (200°C). On a lightly floured surface, roll ⅙ of sugar dough into a round disc about 6 inches (15 cm) in diameter. Place in a 4-inch (10-cm) tart mold and shape edges. In places where the dough breaks or cracks, patch with additional dough to make a smooth surface with no holes. Repeat with rest of dough to line 6 tart pans. Arrange nectarine slices in tart pans.

In a medium bowl, beat together sour cream, sugar, flour, salt, vanilla, and egg. Spoon mixture over nectarines in the tart shells. Bake 15 minutes. With fingers or pastry blender, work together brown sugar, butter, and flour until mixture is crumbly. Sprinkle over tarts, return to oven, and continue baking for another 10 to 15 minutes. Let cool slightly, unmold, and continue to cool on rack. Tarts can be served immediately or stored in refrigerator and served cold.

MAKES 6 4-INCH (10-CM) TARTS.

Chocolate Hazelnut Cookies

⅓ cup (40 g) cocoa powder
1⅔ cups (190 g) all-purpose flour
½ cup (60 g) blanched hazelnuts, finely chopped
pinch salt
¾ cup (150 g) sugar
1 cup (227 g) cold unsalted butter, cut into ½-inch (13-mm) pieces
1 large egg
1 teaspoon vanilla extract
1½ teaspoons cold water

This cookie dough is best when made in a food processor. Place cocoa, flour, hazelnuts, salt, and sugar in the bowl of a food processor. Pulse in butter until mixture resembles coarse meal. Add egg, vanilla, and water. Pulse until a dough forms. Do not overmix. Stop machine as soon as dough comes together. Scrape dough onto plastic wrap and roll into 2 logs 12 inches (30 cm) long. Chill dough for about 30 minutes. When ready to bake cookies, preheat oven to 350°F (180°C). Slice log into ¼-inch (6-mm) rounds. Place on ungreased baking sheets and bake for 10 minutes.

MAKES 6 DOZEN SMALL COOKIES.

Fireside Toasted-Walnut Madeleines

2 ounces (56 g) walnuts
1 cup (227 g) unsalted butter, at room temperature
½ cup (100 g) sugar
3 large eggs
2 tablespoons amaretto liqueur
¼ cup (60 ml) heavy cream
¼ teaspoon almond extract
1⅓ cups (186 g) all-purpose flour
½ teaspoon salt
1 teaspoon baking powder

Preheat oven to 350°F (180°C). Toast walnuts on baking sheet in oven until lightly browned, 5 to 7 minutes. Set aside to cool. Butter miniature madeleine or muffin molds. Place molds in refrigerator. In a medium bowl, cream butter and sugar with an electric mixer until very light and fluffy. Add eggs one at a time, beating after each addition. Add amaretto, cream, and almond extract. Scrape sides of bowl and beat until well combined.

In a blender or food processor grind the walnuts with the flour, salt, and baking powder. Add flour mixture to butter mixture and combine well with wooden spoon or spatula. Fill molds ¾ full with batter. Bake about 12 minutes or until golden brown. Remove from molds immediately.

MAKES ABOUT 4 DOZEN MINIATURE MADELEINES.

Coconut Tuiles

½ cup (100 g) sugar
½ cup (70 g) all-purpose flour
3 large egg whites
½ teaspoon coconut extract
¼ cup (56 g) unsalted butter, melted
½ cup (45 g) unsweetened shredded dried coconut

Preheat oven to 375°F (190°C). Grease baking sheets and place in freezer to chill. In a medium bowl, combine sugar and flour. Stir in egg whites, coconut extract, and melted butter. Combine thoroughly. With the back of a spoon, spread batter very thinly into 3-inch (8-cm) circles on baking sheets. Sprinkle each circle with coconut. Bake until circles are evenly lightly browned, 6 to 7 minutes. Remove from oven. Carefully lift each circle off baking sheet with a thin metal spatula. Drape cookie over a rolling pin or other cylindrical object such as a narrow bottle. Allow to harden (about 2 minutes) and remove.

MAKES ABOUT 20 TUILES.

New World Pecan Bourbon Shortbread

¾ cup (170 g) unsalted butter, at room temperature
¾ cup (100 g) sugar
6 ounces (170 g) pecans, finely ground
1 large egg yolk
¼ teaspoon salt
1 vanilla bean or 1 teaspoon vanilla extract
2 tablespoons bourbon
1½ cups (195 g) all-purpose flour

Cream butter until light, then add sugar and pecans. Beat until fluffy. Add egg yolk and salt. Slice vanilla bean in half and scrape seeds into butter mixture. Add bourbon and beat for 1 minute more, then fold in flour. Wrap dough in plastic wrap and chill for ½ hour.

Preheat oven to 325°F (165°C). Dust work surface with flour and roll dough out ⅓ inch (8 mm) thick. Cut dough into 1 x 2-inch (2 x 5-cm) rectangles. Put cookies on a baking sheet lined with parchment or waxed paper. Bake for about 10 minutes or until very lightly browned. Do not overbake. Let cool before removing from baking sheet.

MAKES 2 DOZEN COOKIES.

Miss Belinda's Apple Syllabub

½ cup (120 ml) sparkling apple cider
2 tablespoons applejack or brandy
¼ cup (50 g) sugar
1 cup (240 ml) heavy cream
¼ teaspoon ground cinnamon

Chill a large mixing bowl in the refrigerator or freezer for 10 minutes. Pour cider, applejack, and sugar into chilled bowl. With a large whisk stir mixture until sugar dissolves. Add heavy cream and cinnamon. Chill for 5 minutes. Beat vigorously with large whisk until cream reaches the consistency of a very thick froth, about 5 to 6 minutes. Stop beating before cream reaches soft peak stage. Ladle syllabub evenly into 4 chilled wineglasses. Serve with pecan shortbread.

MAKES 4 SERVINGS.

Chocolate Brandied-Cherry Christmas Cake

8 ounces (227 g) semisweet or bittersweet chocolate
6 tablespoons (84 g) unsalted butter, at room temperature
3 large eggs, separated
½ cup (100 g) plus 3 tablespoons sugar
¾ cup (90 g) ground lightly toasted almonds
¼ teaspoon almond extract
3 ½ ounces (100 g) cherries in brandy (griottines), drained and coarsely chopped
⅓ cup (80 ml) brandy and juice from cherries
2 tablespoons flour
confectioners' sugar
fresh mint leaves (optional)
sweetened whipped cream

Preheat oven 350°F (180°C). Butter and flour a 9-inch (23-cm) round cake pan. In a small bowl, melt chocolate over barely simmering water. Cut butter into small pieces and stir into chocolate until melted. Beat egg yolks and ½ cup (100 g) sugar with an electric mixer until pale yellow and thick. Slowly beat butter and chocolate mixture into yolks with a wire whisk. Add ground almonds, almond extract, cherries, and brandy. Stir until completely mixed. In a clean bowl, beat egg whites until frothy. Add remaining 3 tablespoons sugar and continue to beat until egg whites are stiff but not dry. Slide whites onto chocolate mixture. Sift flour over egg whites and fold into chocolate gently with a spatula until whites and flour are incorporated.

Fill prepared pan with batter. Bake 25 to 30 minutes, until a toothpick inserted near center of cake comes out clean. Cool cake in pan on cake rack. When cool, remove cake from pan by inverting onto a plate and lifting off pan. Sprinkle with confectioners' sugar and decorate with additional cherries and mint leaves if desired. Serve at room temperature with sweetened whipped cream.

MAKES 1 9-INCH (23-CM) CAKE.

Poached Pear Coupe

½ cup (40 g) sliced blanched almonds
6 poached pear halves (p. 42)
1 quart (1 liter) vanilla ice cream
1 recipe caramel sauce (recipe follows)

Preheat oven to 350°F (180°C). Toast almonds on a baking sheet for about 5 minutes or until golden. Set aside to cool. To assemble sundaes, place each poached pear half in an ice cream dish. Top each with a scoop of ice cream. Drizzle with caramel sauce and sprinkle with toasted almonds. Serve immediately.

MAKES 6 COUPES.

Caramel Sauce

1 cup (200 g) sugar
½ cup (120 ml) water
few drops lemon juice
1¼ cups (300 ml) heavy cream

In a small heavy-bottomed saucepan, place sugar, water, and lemon juice. Cook over high heat until sugar just begins to color. Reduce heat to low and watch sugar carefully now, because caramel can easily burn. Continue to cook until mixture is a dark amber color. Remove from heat and add cream carefully. Sauce will bubble up immediately. Allow to settle. Whisk to make a smooth sauce. If there is any hard caramel, heat on low and whisk to dissolve it. Let cool to lukewarm. Sauce can be made ahead and stored in refrigerator until ready to use. Warm when ready to use if sauce has been in refrigerator.

MAKES 1½ CUPS (360 ML).

Mrs. Cratchit's Baked Pumpkin Pudding

The pudding was out of the copper. A smell like a washing-day! That was the cloth. A smell like an eating-house and a pastrycook's next door to each other, with a laundress's next door to that! That was the pudding! In half a minute Mrs. Cratchit entered—flushed, but smiling proudly—with the pudding, like a speckled cannon-ball, so hard and firm, blazing in half of half-a-quartern of ignited brandy, and bedight with Christmas holly stuck into the top.

1½ cups (210 g) all-purpose flour
1 teaspoon baking soda
1 teaspoon baking powder
1 teaspoon ground ginger
1 teaspoon ground cinnamon
¼ teaspoon salt
½ cup (114 g) unsalted butter, at room temperature
1 cup (200 g) sugar
1 cup (220 g) pumpkin purée
2 large eggs
1 cup (280 g) firmly packed mincemeat (p. 52)
or 1 cup (180 g) chopped dried fruit
whipped cream

Preheat oven to 325°F (165°C). Butter 6 ovenproof 1-cup (240-ml) ramekins. In a small bowl, sift together flour, baking soda, baking powder, ginger, cinnamon, and salt. In a medium bowl, beat together butter and sugar until fluffy. Add pumpkin purée and eggs. Beat until blended. Add mincemeat and continue to beat until mixed. Add dry ingredients and stir until well blended. Spoon into prepared ramekins. Cover ramekins tightly with foil.

Place ramekins in a baking pan and add enough boiling water to reach halfway up sides of ramekins. Bake 1½ hours or until set. Check water level in pan every ½ hour. Let cool 10 minutes and unmold. Serve warm with whipped cream. Pudding can be made ahead and reheated when ready to serve.

MAKES 6 INDIVIDUAL PUDDINGS.

Rhubarb Fool

"I don't know what day of the month it is!" said Scrooge. "I don't know how long I've been among the Spirits. I don't know anything. I'm quite a baby. Never mind. I don't care. I'd rather be a baby. Hallo! Whoop! Hallo here!"

1½ pounds (780 g) rhubarb, sliced into 1-inch (2-cm) chunks
1 cup (200 g) sugar
½ cup (120 ml) water
1 pint (480 ml) heavy cream
1 pint (340 g) fresh raspberries
fresh mint leaves

In a medium heavy-bottomed saucepan, place rhubarb, sugar, and water. Cook over low heat until rhubarb is so soft that, when stirred, it becomes a smooth purée. Let cool. While rhubarb is cooling, whip cream in a medium bowl until soft peaks form. Fold cool rhubarb purée into whipped cream and add raspberries, reserving some for garnish. Spoon into wineglasses and chill until ready to serve. Decorate each glass with reserved raspberries and mint leaves if desired. A fool should be served the same day that it is made.

MAKES 8 SERVINGS.

Apricot Trifle

4 ounces (114 g) dried apricots
¾ cup (180 ml) amaretto liqueur
¾ cup (180 ml) orange juice
5 large egg yolks
½ cup (100 g) sugar
1 tablespoon cornstarch
½ teaspoon almond extract
1¾ cups (320 ml) milk
1 pint (480 ml) heavy cream
1 7-ounce (200 g) package savoiardi biscuits or 18 ladyfingers
6 ounces (170 g) sliced almonds, lightly toasted
12 fresh apricots, pitted and sliced

Place dried apricots, ¾ cup (180 ml) water, amaretto, and orange juice in a medium saucepan. Bring to a boil over low heat. Remove from heat and set aside. In a small bowl, whisk together egg yolks, ¼ cup (50 g) sugar, cornstarch, and almond extract. In a clean medium saucepan, bring milk to a boil. When it comes to a boil, pour a little milk into yolk mixture and whisk to combine. Pour mixture back into saucepan of boiling milk and cook over medium heat, whisking constantly, until mixture just comes to a boil. Transfer to a clean bowl and chill.

Drain soaked apricots, reserving liquid. Purée them with ½ cup (120 ml) water in food processor or blender until smooth. Whisk purée into cooled custard mixture. In a large bowl, beat cream with remaining ¼ cup (50 g) sugar until fairly stiff peaks form. Fold ½ of the whipped cream into the apricot custard mixture. Reserve remaining whipped cream.

Using a 6- to 8-cup (1.5- to 2-liter) glass serving bowl, dip savoiardi biscuits or ladyfingers one by one into reserved liquid from dried apricots. Make sure liquid completely soaks through biscuits. Make a single layer of them on the bottom of the bowl. Spread some of the apricot cream on top of this. Make a layer of fresh apricot slices on top of the cream, and then sprinkle with almonds. Continue layering in this manner until bowl is almost full. Use reserved whipped cream for top layer. Decorate with apricot slices and almonds. Refrigerate at least ½ hour or overnight before serving.

MAKES 10 SERVINGS.

Twelfth-Night Gingerbread Cake

2 cups (280 g) all-purpose flour
1 teaspoon baking soda
1 teaspoon baking powder
1 teaspoon ground cinnamon
2 teaspoons ground ginger
¼ teaspoon ground cloves
¾ cup (170 g) unsalted butter, at room temperature
¾ cup (180 g) dark brown sugar
2 large eggs
½ cup (120 g) sour cream
½ cup (120 ml) molasses
whipped cream or lemon curd (p. 49) (optional)

Preheat oven to 350°F (180°C). Generously butter an 8-inch (30-cm) square cake pan. In a medium bowl, sift together flour, baking soda, baking powder, cinnamon, ginger, and cloves. Set aside. In a large bowl, cream butter and sugar until well blended. Add eggs, sour cream, and molasses. Beat together until blended. Stir in dry ingredients until batter is smooth. Scrape into prepared pan. Bake 40 to 50 minutes or until cake springs back to the touch. Cut cake into squares and serve warm with whipped cream or lemon curd.

MAKES 1 8-INCH (20-CM) SQUARE CAKE.

The Ghost of Christmas Repast

A Plentiful Holiday Feast of Fish, Fowl, and Meat

Heaped up on the floor, to form a kind of throne, were turkeys, geese, game, poultry, brawn, great joints of meat, sucking-pigs, long wreaths of sausages, mince-pies, plum puddings, barrels of oysters, red-hot chestnuts, cherry-cheeked apples, juicy oranges, luscious pears, immense twelfth-cakes, and seething bowls of punch, that made the chamber dim with their delicious steam.

Tiny Tim's Mini Shepherd's Pie

With *A Christmas Carol*, Charles Dickens recreated part of his own childhood. The Cratchit family lived in a small terraced house that evoked the house in Bayham Street where the Dickens family lived after their arrival in London. And Dickens had a crippled young brother whose name was not Tiny Tim but "Tiny Fred."

15 small red potatoes, about 2 pounds (908 g)
salt and freshly ground black pepper
2 tablespoons (28 g) unsalted butter
2 tablespoons milk
6 slices cooked bacon, crumbled
1 cup (100 g) grated sharp Cheddar cheese

Filling

1 tablespoon vegetable oil
1 clove garlic, minced
¾ cup (80 g) finely chopped onions
8 ounces (227 g) ground beef
¼ teaspoon salt
¼ teaspoon freshly ground black pepper
⅛ teaspoon cayenne pepper
1 large egg, lightly beaten

In a large saucepan, boil potatoes in salted water until tender, about 20 minutes. While potatoes are cooking, make the filling. In a medium skillet, heat oil over medium heat. Add garlic and onions and sauté for 3 minutes until onion is translucent. Add ground beef, salt, black pepper and cayenne. Brown meat, then remove skillet from heat. Immediately whisk in egg and set aside.

Preheat oven to 400°F (190°C). When potatoes are cooked, drain. Halve each potato and place on a cookie sheet lined with foil. Scoop out each potato half with a melon baller or spoon. Place scooped center in a bowl. Leave a little potato in the skin for support. Mash potato filling with salt, pepper, butter, and milk until smooth. To assemble, fill potato halves with meat filling. Top with some crumbled bacon, then cover with mashed potatoes and sprinkle with grated cheese. Bake for 10 minutes. Serve immediately.

MAKES 30 HORS D'OEUVRES.

Spectral Stilton Dip

"What evidence would you have of my reality beyond that of your senses?"
"Because," said Scrooge, "a little thing affects them. A slight disorder of the stomach makes them cheats. You may be an undigested bit of beef, a blot of mustard, a crumb of cheese, a fragment of an underdone potato. There's more of gravy than of grave about you, whatever you are!"

½ cup (100 g) crumbled Stilton cheese (or other blue cheese)
1 cup (226 g) sour cream
4 ounces (114 g) cream cheese, at room temperature
¼ cup (10 g) minced fresh chives
salt and freshly ground black pepper

In a small bowl, beat all ingredients until well blended. Season with salt and pepper to taste. Chill until ready to use. Dip is best made several hours to 1 day in advance to allow flavors to blend. Serve dip with a basket of assorted raw vegetables.

MAKES 2 CUPS (450 G).

Martha's Mustard-Encrusted Leg of Lamb

1 leg of lamb, boned and tied, 3 ½ to 4 pounds (1.6 to 1.8 kg)
3 tablespoons olive oil
1 tablespoon salt
1 tablespoon freshly ground black pepper
¼ cup (60 g) Dijon mustard
½ cup (225 g) fresh breadcrumbs
3 cloves garlic, minced
¼ cup (10 g) minced fresh parsley
4 teaspoons minced fresh thyme

Preheat oven to 400°F (200°C). Pat meat dry with paper towels. Rub whole leg with 1 tablespoon oil. Sprinkle with salt and pepper. Heat a large skillet over medium-high heat until very hot, about 2 minutes. Pour remaining 2 tablespoons oil into pan. Sear lamb on all sides over high heat until well browned, about 10 to 15 minutes. Transfer meat to a rack in a large roasting pan. Let cool slightly. Brush all over with Dijon mustard. In a small bowl, combine breadcrumbs, garlic, parsley, and thyme. Pat crumb mixture firmly into mustard coating, covering lamb completely. Roast leg on middle rack of oven until meat thermometer inserted into center of meat reads 125°F (50°C) for medium rare or 135°F (60°C) for medium well, about 1 hour. Remove meat from oven. Let sit for at least 15 minutes before carving. Slice thinly and serve with assorted breads and condiments. Horseradish Sage Mustard (p. 48) and the Onion–Sweet Pepper Relish (p. 41) make great accompaniments.

MAKES 20 APPETIZER SERVINGS.

Fan's Mini Sausage Popovers

"I have come to bring you home, dear brother!" said the child, clapping her tiny hands, and bending down to laugh.
"Home, little Fan?" returned the boy.
"Yes!" said the child, brimful of glee. "Home, for good and all. Home, for ever and ever. Father is so much kinder than he used to be, that home's like Heaven! . . . we're to be together all the Christmas long, and have the merriest time in all the world."

1 pound (454 g) bulk pork breakfast sausage
1 ¼ cups (175 g) all-purpose flour
¼ teaspoon salt
¼ teaspoon freshly ground black pepper
½ teaspoon minced fresh thyme leaves
2 large eggs
½ cup (120 ml) milk
½ cup (120 ml) buttermilk
2 tablespoons (28 g) unsalted butter, melted

Butter 1½-inch (4-cm) miniature muffin cups and set aside. Preheat oven to 400°F (200°C). Heat a large skillet with ¼ cup (60 ml) water. Add sausage meat and fry over medium-high heat until well browned and cooked through, about 8 to 10 minutes. Break up meat into pieces with a large fork or spatula while frying. Drain sausage on paper towels.

In a medium bowl, combine flour, salt, pepper, and thyme. In another bowl, combine eggs, milk, buttermilk, and melted butter. Make a well in flour mixture. Add liquid ingredients and whisk slowly together until well combined. Batter may be slightly lumpy. Fill muffin cups ¼ full with batter. Place a small piece of sausage on top of batter and fill to top with more batter. Bake until browned, about 20 minutes. Serve immediately.

MAKES 4 DOZEN POPOVERS.

Mrs. Fezziwig's Spicy Chicken

1 ½ pounds (780 g) boneless skinless chicken breasts
1 teaspoon salt
juice of 1 lemon
1 tablespoon freshly grated ginger
1 teaspoon ground cumin
⅛ teaspoon cayenne pepper
1 teaspoon paprika
1 teaspoon curry powder
2 cloves garlic, minced
2 tablespoons honey
8 ounces (227 g) plain low-fat or nonfat yogurt

Dipping Sauce

4 ounces (114 g) pitted prunes
8 ounces (227 g) plain low-fat or nonfat yogurt
1 tablespoon honey
1 small red onion, grated
pinch cayenne pepper
salt and freshly ground black pepper

Cut chicken breasts crosswise into 1-inch (2-cm) strips. Place in a shallow dish large enough so that chicken strips are only 1 layer thick. Sprinkle with the salt. In a small bowl, whisk together remaining ingredients (except those for sauce) until well blended. Pour over chicken. Cover dish and refrigerate for at least 4 hours or overnight.

To make dipping sauce, purée prunes in a food processor or blender until they are a smooth paste. Add remaining ingredients and continue to blend until smooth. Pour sauce into a small bowl and refrigerate until ready to serve.

Preheat oven to 400°F (200°C). Spread chicken strips on a baking sheet and bake for 10 minutes. Then turn on broiler and broil chicken for 3 to 5 minutes or until cooked through and browned. Chicken may also be placed on skewers and grilled. Serve warm with dipping sauce.

MAKES 2 DOZEN CHICKEN STRIPS.

Hot Crab Spread

8 ounces (227 g) cream cheese, at room temperature
1 tablespoon milk
8 ounces crabmeat (227 g), cleaned and drained
2 tablespoons finely chopped onion
¼ teaspoon salt
⅛ teaspoon freshly ground black pepper
3 tablespoons minced fresh parsley

Mix all ingredients except parsley in a small bowl. Stir to blend. Place mixture in an ovenproof dish. Bake for 10 to 12 minutes at 375°F (190°C) until hot. Sprinkle with minced parsley. Serve hot with sliced bread or crackers.

MAKES 6 TO 8 SERVINGS.

Horn of Plenty Potted Shrimp

2 tablespoons (28 g) unsalted butter
8 ounces (227 g) raw shrimp, shelled and deveined
½ teaspoon shellfish seasoning
¼ teaspoon salt
¼ teaspoon freshly ground black pepper
¼ cup (30 g) finely chopped scallions
1 tablespoon brandy
2 tablespoons minced fresh dill
2 tablespoons heavy cream

In a large skillet, melt butter over medium heat. Add shrimp, shellfish seasoning, salt, and pepper. Cook, stirring constantly, for 2 minutes. Add scallions and cook for another minute. Stir in brandy, dill, and cream and cook 2 minutes. Pour mixture into a bowl and let cool. Remove shrimp and chop finely with a sharp knife. Return to bowl and combine well. Pack shrimp mixture lightly into 3-ounce (90-ml) ramekins or a larger crock. Cover tightly and chill. Serve as a spread on buttered whole-grain toast.

MAKES 3 3-OUNCE (90-ML) RAMEKINS.

Vegetable Mousse Terrine

2 tablespoons (28 g) unsalted butter
2 medium onions, diced
½ cup (120 ml) heavy cream
½ cup (120 ml) water
1 large potato, peeled and diced (about 1 cup/140 g)
2 cups (250 g) thinly sliced carrots
1 teaspoon salt
¼ teaspoon freshly ground black pepper
pinch ground nutmeg
2 cups (220 g) broccoli florets, steamed until tender, or defrosted and drained if frozen
3 large eggs, lightly beaten
mixed steamed vegetables for decoration, such as extra broccoli florets, julienned carrots, or leeks (optional)

Preheat oven to 350°F (180°C). Butter a 5-cup (1.25-liter) terrine mold or loaf pan. Line pan with waxed paper and butter waxed paper. Set aside. In a medium skillet, melt butter over medium heat. Add onions and cook until they begin to color, about 5 minutes. Add cream, water, potato, carrots, salt, pepper, and nutmeg. Bring to boil. Reduce heat, cover, and let simmer until vegetables are tender, 20 to 25 minutes. Let mixture cool slightly.

Purée mixture in a blender or food processor. Add broccoli florets and continue to blend until smooth. In a large bowl, whisk together vegetable purée with eggs until well blended. Pour into prepared mold. Set mold into a pan of warm water and place on middle rack of oven. Bake for about 1 hour or until toothpick inserted in center comes out clean and terrine has set. Let cool in pan of water.

Chill in refrigerator until ready to serve. To serve, unmold onto a large serving plate and garnish with steamed vegetables if desired. Serve with bread or crackers.

MAKES 1 5-CUP (1.25-LITER) LOAF.

Ali Baba's Anchovy Sticks

"Why, it's Ali Baba!" Scrooge exclaimed in ecstasy. *"It's dear old honest Ali Baba! Yes, yes, I know! One Christmas time, when yonder solitary child was left here all alone, he did come, for the first time, just like that."*

1 pound (454 g) prepared puff pastry
1 large egg yolk
12 anchovy fillets, rinsed, drained, and cut in half lengthwise

Line a baking sheet with waxed paper or parchment. On a lightly floured surface, roll 8 ounces (227 g) puff pastry into a rectangle 12 x 9 inches (30 x 23 cm). Place on baking sheet. In a small bowl, mix egg yolk with 2 tablespoons water. Whisk with fork to blend. Brush pastry lightly with egg mixture. Evenly place anchovy fillets over surface of pastry, about ¾ inch apart. On a lightly floured surface, roll remaining 8 ounces (227 g) puff pastry into a rectangle the same size as the first one. Place on top of anchovies and press gently around edges to seal pastry. Brush surface with egg mixture. With a sharp knife, cut pastry into 12 pieces across and then in half. There should be 24 strips measuring 1 x 4½ inches (2 x 11.5 cm). Place baking sheets with anchovy sticks in freezer for 10 minutes. Meanwhile, preheat oven to 400°F (200°C). After anchovy sticks have chilled, bake them for about 20 minutes, until golden and crisp.

MAKES 24 STICKS.

Cabbage and Leek Pasties

Dough

1 ½ cups (210 g) all-purpose flour
1 teaspoon salt
¼ teaspoon freshly ground black pepper
½ cup (114 g) cold unsalted butter, cut into ½-inch (13-mm) pieces
3 tablespoons milk
1 teaspoon white vinegar

Filling

⅓ cup (70 g) chopped bacon
⅓ cup (40 g) chopped leeks
2 ½ cups (8 ounces/227 g) shredded cabbage
½ teaspoon salt
⅛ teaspoon freshly ground black pepper
⅛ teaspoon paprika
⅛ cup (60 ml) water
¼ cup (60 ml) heavy cream

To make dough, combine flour, salt, and pepper in a medium bowl. Cut in butter until mixture resembles coarse meal. Combine milk and vinegar in a small bowl. Make a well in the center of the flour mixture. Pour milk mixture slowly into center of well and stir until liquid is incorporated and a dough is formed. Wrap dough in plastic wrap and refrigerate.

Meanwhile, make the filling. Fry bacon in a large skillet over low heat until lightly browned but not completely cooked. Add leeks, cabbage, salt, pepper, and paprika. Sauté for 2 minutes. Add water and cream. Cover skillet and cook over low heat until vegetables are soft, 10 to 15 minutes. Transfer filling to a bowl. Cool to room temperature and then refrigerate.

When dough and filling are both chilled, preheat oven to 350°F (180°C). Line a baking sheet with parchment or waxed paper. Roll dough on a floured surface to ¼ inch (6 mm) thick. Cut into 2½-inch (6-cm) rounds. Place 1 tablespoon of filling on each round. With a pastry brush, brush edges of dough lightly with water. Fold over into a half-moon shape and press rounded edge with tines of a fork to seal. Brush each pastry with a little additional heavy cream. Arrange on baking sheet and bake 20 minutes, until bottoms are browned.

MAKES ABOUT 20 PASTIES.

Founder of the Feast Gravalax

1 side salmon (2 to 3 pounds/1 to 1.5 kg), boned and cleaned, skin on
6 ounces (170 g) coarse sea salt
½ cup (100 g) sugar
½ teaspoon ground white pepper
1 tablespoon crushed pink peppercorns
1 tablespoon fennel seeds
¼ teaspoon dry mustard
3 large bunches fresh dill, washed
1 cup (240 ml) olive oil

Place salmon in a pan large enough for the fillet to lie flat. Mix salt, sugar, white pepper, pink peppercorns, fennel seeds, and dry mustard in a small bowl. Coarsely chop 1 bunch dill and add to bowl. Press mixture evenly on both sides of salmon fillet. Put less of mixture on tail where fillet is thinner. Spread 1 bunch of dill (whole sprigs) over top of salmon. Cover pan and refrigerate for 24 hours.

Remove from refrigerator and rinse salmon under cold tap water. Place in a large pan of cold water and continuously run a thin stream of cold water into pan to wash salmon for 20 minutes. Dry between 2 towels. Line a baking sheet with plastic wrap. Lay dill sprigs on plastic and sprinkle evenly with ½ cup (120 ml) olive oil. Lay salmon on top of dill and olive oil. Spread remaining dill and ½ cup (120 ml) olive oil evenly over top of fillet. Wrap tightly and refrigerate.

Daily unwrap fish and turn to keep moist and coated with oil. Rewrap and refrigerate. The salmon will keep 5 to 7 days and can be served at any point after it is wrapped with the oil and dill. To serve, slice thinly and accompany with sliced bread and side dishes of mustard, finely diced onion, capers, and lemon. Gravalax is also delicious in tea sandwiches.

MAKES 1 CURED SIDE OF SALMON.

Baked Oysters Remoulade

24 fresh oysters

Remoulade
½ cup (110 g) prepared mayonnaise
1 tablespoon whole-grain mustard
¼ teaspoon cayenne pepper
¼ teaspoon paprika
1 teaspoon lemon juice
2 tablespoons diced cornichons
2 tablespoons minced fresh parsley
1 tablespoon prepared horseradish
salt and freshly ground black pepper
1½ cups chopped cooked spinach, drained, or
1 10-ounce package frozen spinach, thawed

Topping
½ cup (60 g) breadcrumbs
½ cup (60 g) grated Parmesan cheese
½ cup (40 g) cooked crumbled bacon
1 teaspoon paprika

Preheat oven to 400°F (200°C). Open oysters and pour juice into a small saucepan. Detach oyster from shell with a sharp knife. Clean bottom of shells and wipe any grit from oysters. Place oysters in a small bowl in refrigerator while preparing remoulade. In a medium bowl, stir together all ingredients for remoulade. Add spinach and mix. Set aside.

To make topping, simmer juice from oysters over medium heat until reduced by half. Strain into a small bowl through a piece of cheesecloth. Add remaining ingredients for topping and stir until blended.

Evenly divide remoulade spinach mixture between the 24 oyster shell bottoms. Make a well in center of each shell and place 1 oyster in each. Sprinkle evenly with topping and press lightly. Arrange oysters on a baking sheet. Bake 10 to 15 minutes, until topping is golden brown. Serve warm with a napkin and a small spoon to get all the juice.

MAKES 24 OYSTERS.

The Ghost of Christmas Presents

Preserves, Candies, and other Edible Gifts

But now a knocking at the door was heard, and such a rush immediately ensued that she with laughing face and plundered dress was borne towards it the center of a flushed and boisterous group, just in time to greet the father, who came home attended by a man laden with Christmas toys and presents. Then the shouting and the struggling, and the onslaught that was made on the defenceless porter! The scaling him with chairs for ladders to dive into his pockets, despoil him of brown-paper parcels, hold on tight by his cravat, hug him round his neck, pommel his back, and kick his legs in irrepressible affection!

Canning Information

These general canning instructions are for recipes like the ones in this book—recipes using foods that are high in acid and therefore can be canned without a pressure cooker. Use Mason jars to obtain a good seal, making sure the edges are smooth and even.

1. *Wash jars and place in a large pot. Sterilize jars by pouring boiling water over them. Let stand in hot water until ready to be filled.*

2. *Meanwhile, place a rack for holding jars in a large, deep kettle. Fill kettle two-thirds full of water and bring to a boil.*

3. *Fill sterilized jars with food, which should be at boiling temperature. Leave ½ inch (13 mm) of space between top of food and rim of each jar.*

4. *Wipe each rim with a damp clean cloth.*

5. *Place lids lightly on jars and, with canning tongs, lower jars onto rack in kettle. Make sure jars do not touch each other.*

6. *Water level should be 1 to 2 inches (2 to 5 cm) above tops of jars. Cover kettle and return water to a rolling boil.*

7. *Begin timing and boil for 10 minutes.*

8. *Remove jars to a rack to cool completely.*

9. *When cool, check seal by pressing on center of each lid. If dip in lid holds, jar is properly sealed. If it bounces back, jar is not sealed.*

10. *Label and date jars. Store in a cool, dry place.*

Onion–Sweet Pepper Relish

*There were ruddy, brown-faced, broad-girthed Spanish Onions,
shining in the fatness of their growth like Spanish Friars, and
winking from their shelves in wanton slyness at the girls as they
went by, and glanced demurely at the hung-up mistletoe.*

3 cups (360 g) chopped onions
3 tablespoons olive oil
½ cup (100 g) sugar
1 teaspoon celery seeds
1 tablespoon all-purpose flour
½ cup (120 ml) cider vinegar
½ teaspoon salt
¼ teaspoon freshly ground black pepper
1 cup (240 ml) water
2 large red bell peppers

In a large heavy-bottomed saucepan, sauté onions in olive oil over medium
heat for about 5 minutes, until translucent. Add sugar and continue to cook
for 3 to 5 minutes, stirring frequently until onions begin to color. Add celery
seeds and flour. Stir to coat onions with flour. Cook for 2 minutes, stirring
constantly. Add vinegar, salt, black pepper, and water. Bring to a boil
over high heat. When mixture boils, reduce heat to low and simmer gently
for 15 minutes.

While simmering, prepare red peppers. To peel, burn skins directly over
flame on gas stove or under broiler until charred. Wrap in foil, let cool,
then peel, seed, and dice. Add to saucepan and continue to simmer relish
for another 15 minutes. Stir occasionally to prevent sticking. Pour into
sterilized jars. Seal and process according to canning instructions (preceding
page) or store in refrigerator for up to 2 weeks.

MAKES 2 CUPS (500 G) RELISH.

Belle's Spiced Poached Pears

6 pears (Anjou, Comice, or Bosc), peeled, halved, and cored
1 bottle (750 ml) Riesling wine
1 ½ cups (300 g) sugar
2 lemons, halved
2 cinnamon sticks
1 vanilla bean, split and scraped, or 1 teaspoon vanilla extract
2 teaspoons whole black peppercorns

Put all ingredients in a large heavy-bottomed saucepan. Add enough water to just cover pears. Depending on pot, water may not be needed. Bring to a boil over medium-high heat. Reduce heat to low and simmer gently for 15 to 20 minutes, until pears are tender but still slightly firm. Spoon pears into sterilized jars and strain poaching liquid over pears to cover them. Seal and process according to canning instructions (p. 40), or let pears cool in liquid and store in refrigerator for up to 2 weeks..

MAKES 12 PEAR HALVES.

Blueberry-Basil Vinegar

Scrooge's nephew revelled in another laugh, and it was impossible to keep the infection off; though the plump sister tried hard to do it with aromatic vinegar; his example was unanimously followed.

3 1/2 cups (840 ml) champagne vinegar
1 cup (20 g) fresh basil leaves, washed and drained
1 1/2 cups (180 g) blueberries, washed and drained
3 tablespoons sugar

Place all ingredients in a 1-quart (1-liter) bottle. Let marinate for 2 weeks. After 2 weeks, bring vinegar to a boil in a medium saucepan. Strain and discard basil and blueberries. Pour strained vinegar into a sterilized 1-quart (1-liter) jar. Add a few blueberries or fresh basil leaves for decoration if desired. Seal jar.

MAKES 1 QUART (1 LITER) VINEGAR.

Port-Marinated Fruit for the New Year

1 bottle (1 liter) ruby port
1/2 cup (100 g) sugar
juice and zest of 1 orange
juice and zest of 1 lemon
1 bay leaf
1 vanilla bean, split and scraped
1 pound (454 g) mixed dried fruit (pears, apricots, prunes, apples, and figs)

Pour port into a large nonaluminum saucepan. Add remaining ingredients except fruit. Bring to a boil, reduce heat, and let simmer 2 minutes. Remove from heat and add fruit. Pour into clean glass jars and let marinate 1 week before eating. If storing for several months, keep refrigerated.

Note: Do not use dried fruit that has sugar added.

MAKES 1 POUND (454 G) FRUIT.

Spirit's Candied Kumquats

"Have you had many brothers, Spirit?"
"More than eighteen hundred," said the Ghost.
"A tremendous family to provide for!" muttered Scrooge.

1 pound (454 g) fresh kumquats
1 ½ cups (300 g) sugar
1 ½ cups (360 ml) water
sugar for coating kumquats

Prick each kumquat several times with a toothpick or tip of a sharp knife. Bring kumquats to a boil in a saucepan filled with water. When water boils, drain kumquats. Return kumquats to saucepan and add sugar and 1 ½ cups (360 ml) water. Bring to a boil over high heat. Reduce heat and simmer for 45 minutes. Drain kumquats, reserving sugar syrup, and set aside.

Return syrup to pan and boil vigorously for 7 to 10 minutes or until thickened. Spoon kumquats into a sterilized jar and fill jar with thickened sugar syrup. Seal tightly and store at room temperature. When ready to serve, drain kumquats for several minutes and roll in granulated sugar.

MAKES 1 POUND (454 G) CANDIED FRUIT.

Dickens and Christmas

Christmas as we know it has its roots in Victorian and specifically Dickensian tradition. Before this time, Christmas was a quiet one-day affair, but Dickens emphasized the festive and joyful part of the holiday. Christmas cards first came into existence in England three years after *A Christmas Carol* was released.

Citrus Marmalade

2 pink grapefruit
2 Temple oranges
2 blood oranges or 2 more Temple oranges
2 tangerines
1 lemon, quartered
3 cups (600 g) sugar

With a knife, peel grapefruit, oranges, and tangerines. Reserve orange and tangerine peels and discard grapefruit peel. Over a large saucepan, section peeled fruit. Place sections and juice in saucepan. Squeeze any juice left in membranes of fruit. Discard seeds and membranes. Add lemon and sugar. Set aside.

Cut reserved peel into thin julienne strips. In a small saucepan filled with cold water, bring peel to a boil. Drain immediately. Refill saucepan with cold water and bring peel to a boil again. Let peel simmer for 3 to 5 minutes, until tender. Drain peel and add to saucepan with fruit and sugar. Add 1 cup (240 ml) water. Bring mixture to a boil. Simmer for 45 minutes to 1 hour, until marmalade thickens.

To test for doneness, place a small plate in refrigerator or freezer until chilled. Spoon a teaspoon of hot marmalade onto chilled plate. Return plate to refrigerator for 5 minutes to cool. This will be consistency of marmalade when it has cooled. If marmalade is too runny, continue to cook until it reaches desired consistency. Remove lemon. Spoon hot marmalade into prepared jars. Seal and process accourding to canning instructions (p. 40), or cover tightly and store in refrigerator for up to 2 months.

MAKES ABOUT 4 CUPS (1,120 G).

Candied Ginger

1 pound (454 g) fresh ginger, peeled and sliced ¼ inch (6 mm) thick
2 cups (400 g) sugar
2 cups (480 ml) water

Place ginger slices in a medium heavy-bottomed saucepan and add enough cold water to cover. Bring to a boil over high heat. Reduce heat and simmer gently for about 2 hours, until ginger slices are tender. Drain ginger and discard water. Return ginger to saucepan and add sugar and 2 cups (480 ml) water. Bring to a boil over high heat. Reduce heat and simmer for 2 hours or until liquid has become a thick syrup. During the 2 hours, if there is not enough liquid, add water as needed. Pour ginger with syrup into a sterilized jar. Seal and process according to canning instructions (p. 40), or store in syrup for up to 2 months.

Ginger in syrup can be used in recipes that call for candied ginger. The syrup can also be used to flavor drinks and cakes. If you do not want to store ginger in syrup, the ginger can be cooled, drained for several hours, and then rolled in sugar. It will keep for several months in a sealed jar and looks prettier to give as a gift.

MAKES 1 POUND (454 G) CANDIED GINGER.

Mango Chutney

2 tablespoons olive oil
2 medium onions, diced
⅓ cup (70 g) sugar (if mangoes are very sweet, reduce sugar slightly)
2 teaspoons ground cumin
2 teaspoons ground coriander
½ teaspoon salt
¼ teaspoon freshly ground black pepper
4 mangoes, peeled and diced
3 tablespoons cider vinegar
½ cup (120 ml) water
1 tablespoon grated fresh ginger
1 cup (150 g) dark raisins

Heat olive oil in a large heavy-bottomed skillet. Add onions and sauté over medium heat until translucent, about 3 minutes. Add sugar and continue to cook 3 to 5 minutes, stirring frequently. Add cumin, coriander, salt, and pepper. Cook 2 minutes, stirring constantly. Add mangoes, vinegar, water, and ginger. Bring to a boil. Reduce heat and simmer gently in partially covered saucepan. After 15 minutes, add raisins. Continue to simmer until liquid has evaporated and chutney has thickened slightly, about 15 more minutes. Spoon into sterilized jars. Seal and process according to canning instructions (p. 40), or refrigerate in a tightly sealed jar for up to 2 weeks.

MAKES 4 CUPS (1,200 G).

Master Peter's Pickled Vegetables

¼ cup (50 g) plus 2 tablespoons salt
1 pound (454 g) Kirby cucumbers, cut into thick slices
1 head cauliflower, broken into florets (2 pounds/908 g florets)
1 red bell pepper, seeded and thinly sliced
2 cups (480 ml) cider vinegar
3 tablespoons pickling spices
1½ cups (300 g) sugar

In a large nonaluminum bowl, mix ¼ cup (50 g) salt with 6 cups (1.5 liters) cold water, cucumbers, cauliflower, and bell pepper. Cover and let marinate overnight. Drain and rinse vegetables and arrange in 2 sterilized 1-quart (1-liter) jars. In a small saucepan, bring 2 tablespoons salt, vinegar, pickling spices, sugar, and ¾ cup (180 ml) water to a boil. Let simmer 1 minute. Pour hot liquid into jars filled with vegetables. Seal and process according to canning instructions (p. 40), or store refrigerated in brine for up to 1 month.

MAKES 2 QUARTS (2 LITERS).

Horseradish Sage Mustard

½ cup (85 g) mustard seeds
½ cup (120 ml) cider vinegar
½ cup (35 g) dry mustard
1 tablespoon prepared horseradish
¼ cup (75 g) honey
1 teaspoon salt
1 tablespoon minced fresh sage or 2 teaspoons dried sage

In a small bowl, mix mustard seeds with vinegar. Let soak for ½ hour. In a small saucepan, combine all ingredients except fresh sage. Add ½ cup (120 ml) water. Whisk to blend. Bring mustard to boil over medium heat. Reduce heat and simmer gently for 5 minutes. Stir in minced sage and let cool. Blend in food processor or blender for 15 seconds, until mustard is creamy but still grainy. Spoon into sterilized jars and process according to canning instructions (p. 40), or store in refrigerator in a tightly sealed jar for up to 2 months.

MAKES 1 ½ CUPS (1.4 KG).

Humbug Lemon Curd

"Bah!" said Scrooge, "Humbug!"
"Christmas a humbug, uncle!" said Scrooge's nephew. "You don't mean that, I am sure?"
"I do," said Scrooge. "Merry Christmas! What right have you to be merry? You're poor enough."
"Come, then," returned the nephew gaily. "What right have you to be dismal? What reason have you to be morose? You're rich enough."

6 large eggs
2 ½ cups (300 g) sugar
grated zest of 4 lemons
1 ½ cups (360 g) fresh lemon juice
1 ½ cups (340 g) unsalted butter

In a medium bowl, whisk together eggs and sugar until well blended. Add lemon zest and juice and mix well. Cut butter into pieces and add to egg mixture. Place bowl over a pot of simmering water. Make sure bowl fits snugly over pot. Cook mixture, whisking occasionally, for about 2 hours or until lemon curd reaches the consistency of lightly whipped cream. Maintain water in pot at half full. Strain curd through a fine sieve into a clean bowl. Pour into sterilized jars. Seal and process according to canning instructions (p. 40), or chill for at least 4 hours before using. Keeps 1 week in refrigerator.

MAKES 5 CUPS (1.5 KG).

Counting-House Creamy Caramels

1 cup (200 g) sugar
1 cup (240 ml) light corn syrup
1 can (14 ounces/420 ml) sweetened condensed milk
1½ cups (360 ml) heavy cream
2 teaspoons pure vanilla extract

Grease an 8-inch (20-cm) square pan. Set aside. In a medium heavy-bottomed pot, bring sugar and corn syrup to a boil, stirring to dissolve sugar. Add condensed milk and cream. Cook over medium-low heat, stirring frequently to prevent caramel from becoming granular. Boil gently (otherwise mixture will boil over) until a candy thermometer reaches 244°F (118° C). Remove from heat. Stir in vanilla and pour into prepared pan. Let cool completely. Cut into squares with a sharp knife. Wrap caramels in plastic wrap or waxed paper. Store in a cool dry place.

MAKES 64 1-INCH (2-CM) CARAMELS.

Chocolate-Covered Toffee

1 cup (200 g) dark brown sugar
2 tablespoons molasses
1 tablespoon white wine vinegar or cider vinegar
¼ cup (60 ml) dark corn syrup
2 tablespoon water
6 tablespoons (84 g) unsalted butter
pinch salt
6 ounces (170 g) semisweet or bittersweet chocolate, melted
6 ounces (170 g) ground walnuts or pecans

Lightly oil a 12 x 17-inch (30 x 43-cm) baking pan. Combine sugar, molasses, vinegar, corn syrup, water, butter, and salt in a large heavy-bottomed pot. Bring to a boil and cook over medium heat until mixture reaches 300°F (150°C) on a candy thermometer (hard crack stage). Carefully pour mixture into oiled pan, spreading thinly and evenly with a metal spatula. Allow to harden completely, about 45 minutes. Break toffee into pieces. With a pastry brush coat each piece of toffee on one side with melted chocolate. Sprinkle with nuts while chocolate is still soft. Allow to set. Toffee can be stored in freezer.

MAKES 1½ POUNDS (680 G).

Ginger Biscuits

½ cup (114 g) unsalted butter, at room temperature
½ cup (100 g) sugar
1 teaspoon vanilla extract
2 tablespoons candied ginger, finely chopped
½ teaspoon ground ginger
1 cup (140 g) all-purpose flour

In a medium bowl, beat butter and sugar until light and creamy. Add vanilla, candied ginger, and ground ginger. Continue to beat until well blended. Fold flour into batter until just incorporated. Wrap dough in plastic wrap or foil and chill for 20 minutes or longer.

When ready to bake cookies, preheat oven to 350°F (180°C). Roll dough on a lightly floured surface to ⅛-inch (3-mm) thickness. Use a 2- to 3-inch (5- to 8-cm) cookie cutter of any shape to cut dough. Place cookies on ungreased baking sheets. Bake 10 to 12 minutes, until lightly browned. Cool cookies on wire rack. Store in a sealed tin in a cool, dry place.

MAKES ABOUT 2 DOZEN COOKIES.

Mincemeat

8 ounces (227 g) dried figs, chopped
8 ounces (227 g) dried apricots, chopped
8 ounces (227 g) prunes, chopped
8 ounces (227 g) dark raisins
2 teaspoons ground cinnamon
1 teaspoon ground ginger
½ teaspoon ground nutmeg
¼ teaspoon ground allspice
¼ teaspoon freshly ground black pepper
1 cup (240 ml) brandy
1 cup (240 ml) cream sherry
½ cup (5½ ounces/164 g) apricot preserves

In a large bowl, combine figs, apricots, prunes, and raisins. In another bowl, whisk spices with brandy and sherry until well blended. Add this mixture to dried fruit along with apricot preserves. Mix well. Spoon into sterilized jars and seal and process according to canning instructions (p. 40), or refrigerate in a tightly sealed jar for up to 4 months.

MAKES 5 CUPS (1.4 KG).

Nephew Fred's Mincemeat Pound Cake

"There are many things from which I might have derived good, by which I have not profited, I dare say," returned the nephew. "Christmas among the rest. But I am sure I have always thought of Christmas time . . . as a good time; a kind, forgiving, charitable, pleasant time; the only time I know of, in the long calendar of the year, when men and women seem by one consent to open their shut-up hearts freely, and to think of people below them as if they

really were fellow-passengers to the grave, and not another race of creatures bound on other journeys. And therefore, uncle, though it has never put a scrap of gold or silver in my pocket, I believe that it has done me good, and will do me good; and I say, God bless it!"

½ cup (114 g) unsalted butter
½ cup (120 g) brown sugar
⅓ cup (65 g) granulated sugar
2 large eggs
½ cup (60 ml) buttermilk
1 cup (280 g) mincemeat (preceding recipe)
1¾ cups (245 g) all-purpose flour
¾ teaspoon baking soda
¼ teaspoon salt

Preheat oven to 350°F (180°C). Butter and flour a 5-cup (1.25-liter) loaf pan. In a large bowl, cream butter, brown sugar, and granulated sugar with an electric mixer until light and fluffy. Beat in eggs one at a time. Scrape sides of bowl. Beat in buttermilk and mincemeat.

In a small bowl, sift flour, baking soda, and salt. Fold sifted dry ingredients into mincemeat mixture with a spatula until smooth. Spoon batter into prepared loaf pan and bake for about 45 minutes, until wooden pick or knife inserted into center comes out clean. Remove cake from pan and cool on rack. Wrap tightly. Cake can be made ahead and frozen until ready to give as a gift.

MAKES 1 LOAF.

The Spirits of Christmas Yet to Come

Tasty Libations for Twelfth-Night

"He has given us plenty of merriment, I am sure," said Fred, "and it would be ungrateful not to drink his health. Here is a glass of mulled wine ready to our hand at the moment; and I say, 'Uncle Scrooge!'"
"Well! Uncle Scrooge!" they cried.
"A Merry Christmas and a Happy New Year to the old man, whatever he is!" said Scrooge's nephew.

Golden Hot Buttered Rum

*"And how did little Tim behave?" asked Mrs. Cratchit, when she
had rallied Bob on his credulity, and Bob had hugged his daughter
to his heart's content.*
"As good as gold," said Bob, "and better."

2 cups (480 ml) apple cider
1 cinnamon stick
2 tablespoons honey
1 tablespoon lemon juice
½ cup (120 ml) dark rum
2 tablespoons (28 g) cold unsalted butter

In a small saucepan, heat cider, cinnamon stick, honey, and lemon juice over
low heat. Bring slowly to a boil and let simmer for 2 minutes. Meanwhile,
pour ¼ cup (60 ml) rum in each of 2 mugs. When cider is ready, pour into
mugs. Discard cinnamon stick. Top each drink with 1 tablespoon (14 g) cold
butter. Serve immediately.

MAKES 2 DRINKS.

Ebenezer's Eggnog

⅓ cup (70 g) vanilla yogurt
3 tablespoons sugar
¼ cup (60 ml) dark rum
¼ cup (60 ml) sherry
1 cup (240 ml) milk
2 large egg whites
½ cup (120 ml) heavy cream
freshly grated nutmeg

In a medium bowl, combine yogurt and sugar. Whisk until sugar dissolves. Add rum, sherry, and milk and combine thoroughly. In another bowl, beat egg whites with an electric mixer until soft peaks form. Slide egg whites onto yogurt mixture but do not mix. In a clean bowl, whip cream until soft peaks form. Gently whisk egg whites and cream into yogurt mixture. Ladle into cups and top with nutmeg.

MAKES 6 6-OUNCE (180-ML) SERVINGS.

Christmas of 1843

Dickens wrote *A Christmas Carol* in only six weeks, finishing in December 1843. Bound in red cloth with a gilt design on the cover and gilt page edges, the book contained four full-color etchings by John Leech and four black-and-white woodcuts. A handsome volume for the relatively low price of five shillings, it became the most successful Christmas book of the season, with 6,000 copies selling by Christmas Eve. Quickly it became a national institution with its own mythology, such as the story of the American factory owner who, on reading the book, gave his employees another day's holiday.

Warm Spiced Claret

4 orange slices
4 cinnamon sticks, broken in half
6 whole cloves
1 bay leaf
4 allspice berries
8 whole black peppercorns
1 bottle (750 ml) dry red wine
¼ cup (50 g) sugar

Place an orange slice in each of 4 large mugs. Wrap spices in a small piece of cheesecloth and tie cheesecloth. In a medium saucepan, bring wine, spices, and sugar to boil. Reduce heat. Keep wine warm but not boiling for 15 minutes to let spices infuse into wine. Serve warm in mugs.

MAKES 4 DRINKS.

Prince Albert's Tea

His tea was ready for him on the hob, and they all tried who should help him to it most.

1 teaspoon jasmine tea leaves or 1 tea bag
2 teaspoons sugar
1½ ounces (45 ml) brandy
2 tablespoons heavy cream
8 dashes bitters

In a teacup, steep tea with 4 ounces (120 ml) boiling water for 2 minutes. If using loose leaves, strain tea. Add sugar, brandy, cream, and bitters. Serve warm.

MAKES 1 DRINK.

Queen Victoria's Iced Tea

The Queen very much wanted to hear a reading of A Christmas Carol. It never came to pass because Dickens felt uncomfortable at the thought of reading it to her alone without an audience to conspire with. Eventually he had his audience with Queen Victoria, who impressed him as "strangely shy" and "like a girl in manner."

3 tablespoons sugar
2 tablespoons minced fresh mint
5 teaspoons tea leaves or 5 tea bags
1 quart (1 liter) ginger ale, chilled
mint sprigs for garnish

In a large bowl, stir together sugar and mint. Add tea leaves to bowl with 4 cups boiling water. Let steep 5 minutes. Strain tea into a pitcher. Chill in refrigerator until ready to serve tea. Fill a tall glass with ice cubes. Pour ½ cup (120 ml) of cold tea into glass, then add ½ cup (120 ml) ginger ale. Place 2 mint sprigs in each glass of iced tea. Serve immediately.

MAKES 8 DRINKS.

Merry Sherry Cocktail

But being thoroughly good-natured, and not much caring what they laughed at, so that they laughed at any rate, he encouraged them in their merriment, and passed the bottle joyously.

1 strip orange peel
2 ounces (60 ml) dry sherry
1 ounce (30 ml) freshly squeezed orange juice, chilled

Rub orange peel around rim of a cocktail glass. Place peel in glass and chill. Pour sherry and orange juice into chilled glass. Stir and serve.

MAKES 1 COCKTAIL.

Old Fezziwig's Mead

In his popular public readings of *A Christmas Carol*,
Dickens impersonated some 23 characters and used
his hands to illustrate the story. During the scene of
the Fezziwigs' party, his hands "actually perform upon
the table, as if it were the floor of Fezziwig's room,
and every finger were a leg belonging to one of the
Fezziwig family."

1 cup (240 ml) dry white wine
⅓ cup (100 g) honey

In a small saucepan, heat wine and honey over low heat until honey is completely dissolved. Pour into a small pitcher or bowl and freeze until wine is ice cold. Serve in small chilled glasses as an after-dinner liqueur.

MAKES 4 DRINKS.

Dover Breeze

1 ounce (30 ml) gin
1 tablespoon cassis liqueur
½ cup (120 ml) grapefruit juice, freshly squeezed

Fill a low-ball or old-fashioned glass with ice. Add gin, cassis, and grapefruit juice to glass. Stir and serve.

MAKES 1 DRINK.

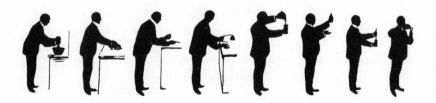

Imperial Gin Cocktail

. . . and while Bob, turning up his cuffs—as if, poor fellow, they were capable of being made more shabby—compounded some hot mixture in jug with gin and lemons, and stirred it round and round and put it on the hob to simmer.

1 ounce (30 ml) lime juice
1 tablespoon sugar
1 teaspoon egg white
2 ounces (60 ml) gin
lime peel

In a cocktail shaker, mix lime juice and sugar. Stir until sugar is dissolved. Because it is difficult to measure 1 teaspoon of egg white, first gently whisk an egg white for a few seconds and then measure 1 teaspoon of egg white into the shaker. Add gin. Add ice cubes and shake until frothy. Strain into a chilled cocktail glass. Garnish with a small piece of lime peel.

MAKES 1 COCKTAIL.

Champagne Punch

½ cup (120 ml) ginger-flavored liqueur
2 cups (480 ml) cranberry juice
1½ cups (360 ml) orange juice
1 orange, thinly sliced
1 lemon, thinly sliced
1 bottle (750 ml) sparkling wine or champagne, chilled

In a chilled bowl, place all ingredients except champagne. Place bowl in freezer until juice begins to freeze, 45 minutes or longer. When ready to serve, remove bowl from freezer and add chilled champagne.

MAKES 8 TO 10 DRINKS.

Haunted Hot Toddy

"You will be haunted," resumed the Ghost, "by Three Spirits."
Scrooge's countenance fell almost as low as the Ghost's had
done. . . .
"Without their visits," said the Ghost, "you cannot hope to shun
the path I tread. Expect the first to-morrow, when the bell tolls
One."
"Couldn't I take 'em all at once, and have it over, Jacob?" hinted
Scrooge.

16 whole cloves
1 lemon, quartered
8 teaspoons sugar
1 cup (240 ml) cognac or scotch whiskey
4 cinnamon sticks

Stick 4 cloves into each lemon quarter and place each quarter into an
8-ounce (240-ml) mug. Add 2 teaspoons of sugar and ¼ cup (60 ml)
cognac or scotch to each mug. Fill with boiling water. Stir with a cinnamon
stick to dissolve sugar and place cinnamon stick in mug. Serve immediately.

MAKES 4 DRINKS.

Merry Christmas Ale

"God bless us every one!" said Tiny Tim, the last of all.

6 ounces (180 ml) pale ale, chilled
1 ounce (30 ml) Chambord liqueur
1 slice lemon

Pour ale and Chambord into a chilled mug. Add lemon slice and serve.

MAKES 1 DRINK.

**Also available in
the Hollywood Hotplates series:**

Gone With The Wind Cookbook ™
The Casablanca Cookbook
The Wizard of Oz Cookbook